# A Cool Yule
## Ten Jazzy Christmas Songs

**Arranged for Intermediate to Advanced Piano**
**By Steve Calderone**

D1307477

# AWAY IN A MANGER

MARTIN LUTHER and CARL MUELLER
*Arranged by* STEVE CALDERONE

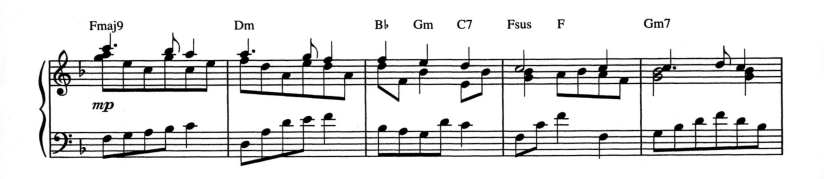

3

4

# DECK THE HALLS

TRADITIONAL WELSH AIR
*Arranged by STEVE CALDERONE*

# THE FIRST NOEL

ENGLISH TRADITIONAL
*Arranged by STEVE CALDERONE*

# GOD REST YE MERRY, GENTLEMEN

ENGLISH TRADITIONAL
*Arranged by STEVE CALDERONE*

**Driving, with intensity**

God Rest Ye Merry, Gentlemen - 5 - 5
AF9832

# GOOD KING WENCESLAS

TRADITIONAL
JOHN NEALE
*Arranged by STEVE CALDERONE*

# HERE WE COME A'WASSAILING

YORKSHIRE
TRADITIONAL
*Arranged by STEVE CALDERONE*

Here We Come A'Wassailing - 4 - 1
AF9832

26

Here We Come A'Wassailing - 4 - 3
AF9832

# LO, HOW A ROSE E'ER BLOOMING/
# O THOU JOYFUL DAY

MICHAEL PRAETORIUS

SICILIAN HYMN
(O SANCTISSIMA)
*Arranged by STEVE CALDERONE*

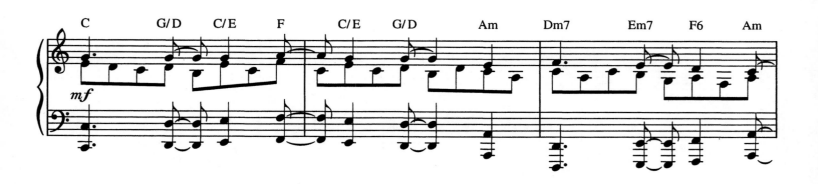

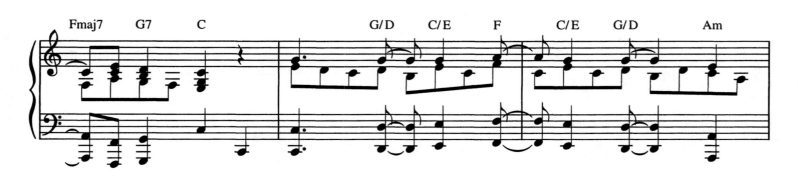

Lo, How a Rose E'er Blooming/O Thou Joyful Day - 6 - 1
AF9832

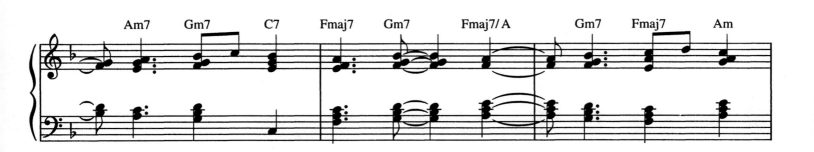

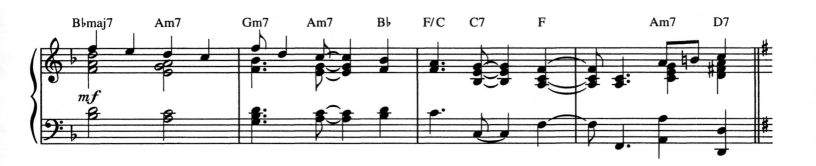

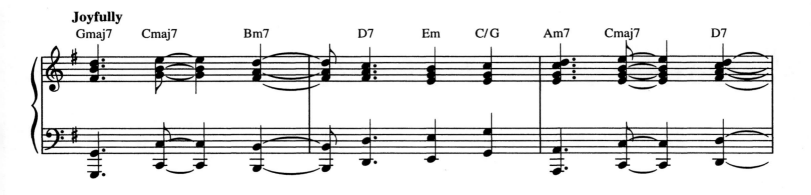

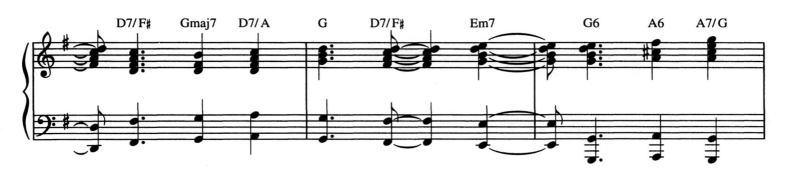

Lo, How a Rose E'er Blooming/O Thou Joyful Day - 6 - 4
AF9832

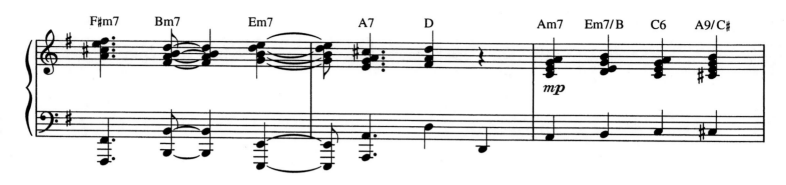

Lo, How a Rose E'er Blooming/O Thou Joyful Day - 6 - 5
AF9832

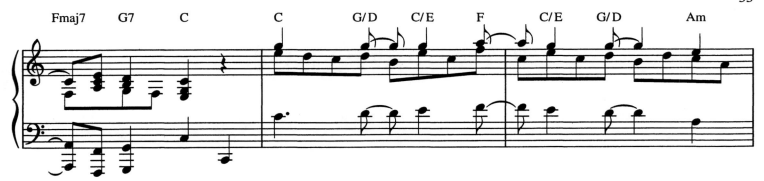

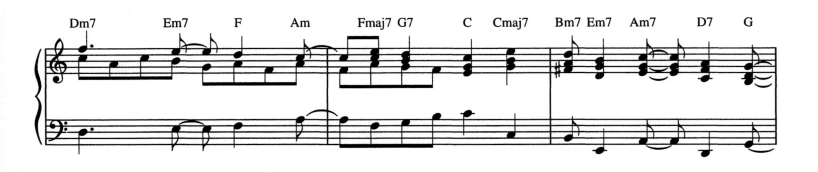

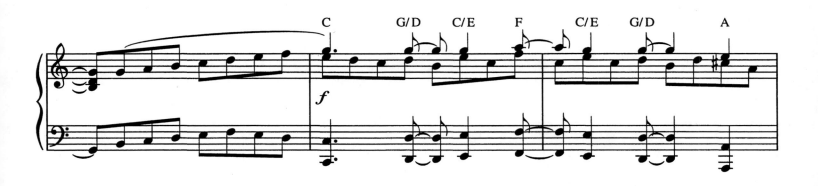

Lo, How a Rose E'er Blooming/O Thou Joyful Day - 6 - 6
AF9832

# O COME ALL YE FAITHFUL

FREDERICK OAKLEY and JOHN READING
*Arranged by* STEVE CALDERONE

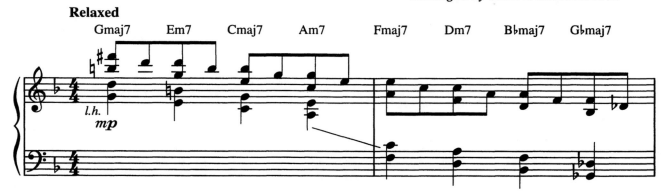

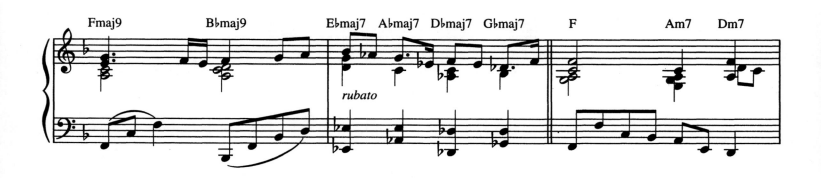

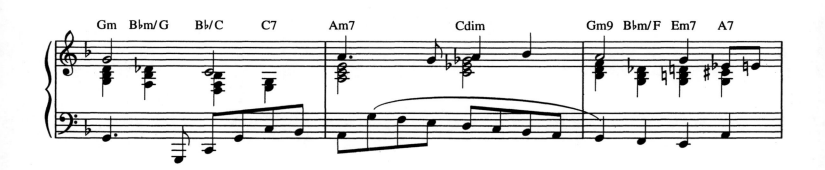

O Come All Ye Faithful - 5 - 1
AF9832

36

# SILENT NIGHT

JOSEPH MOHR and FRANZ GRUBER
*Arranged by STEVE CALDERONE*

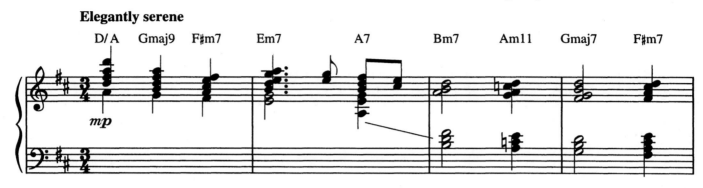

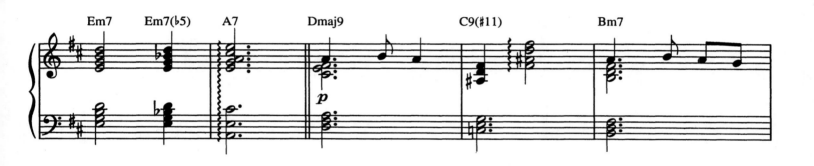

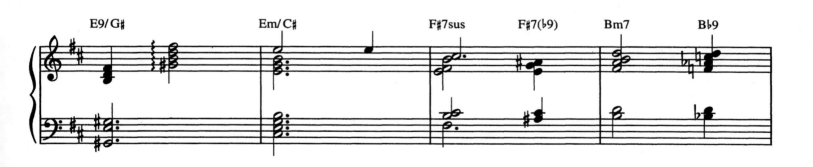

# WHAT CHILD IS THIS?

WILLIAM C. DIX
TRADITIONAL ENGLISH
GREENSLEEVES
*Arranged by STEVE CALDERONE*

What Child Is This? - 5 - 2
AF9832

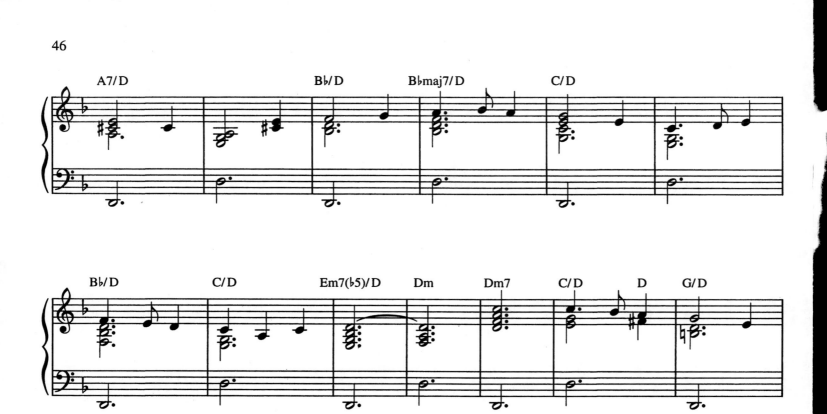

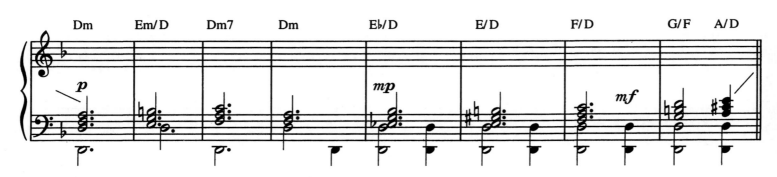

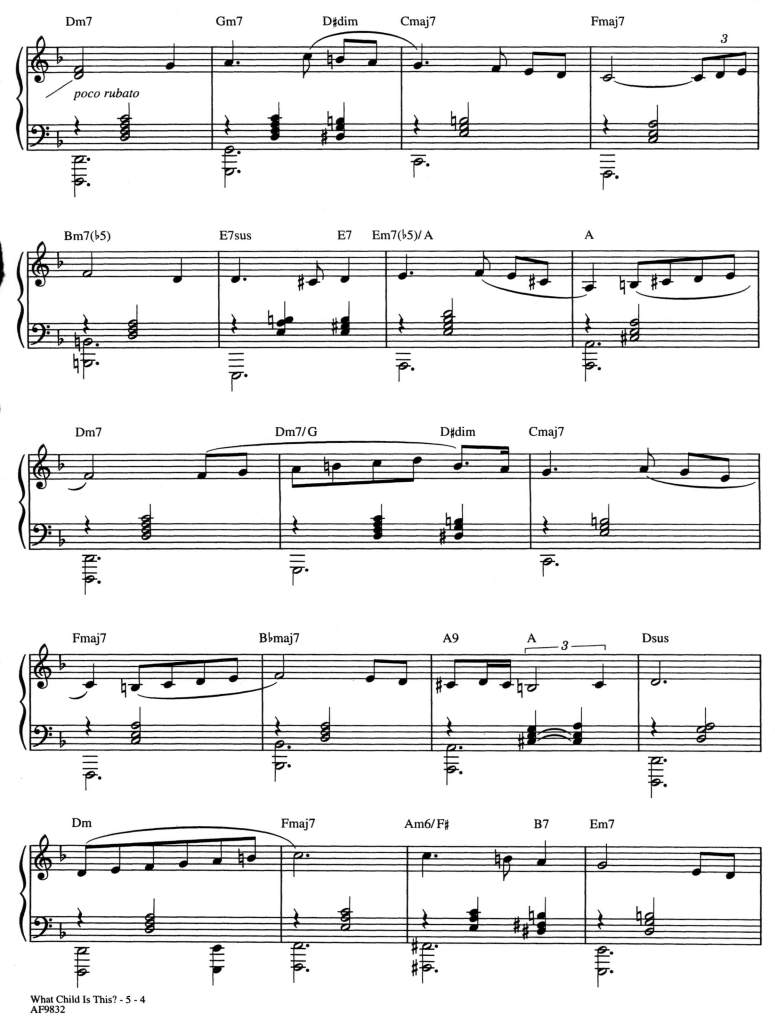

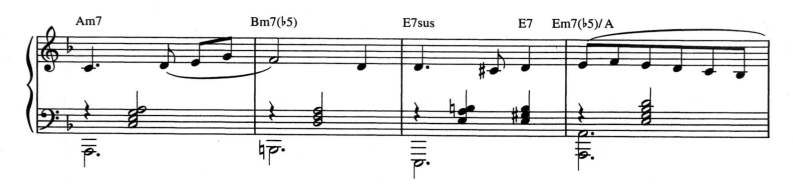

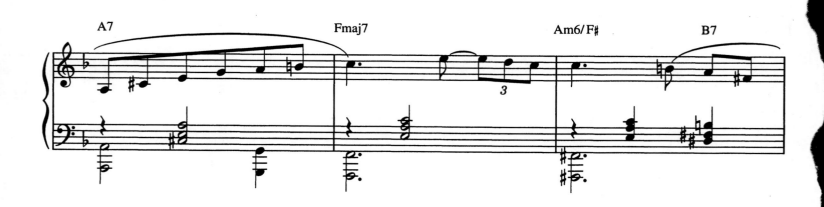

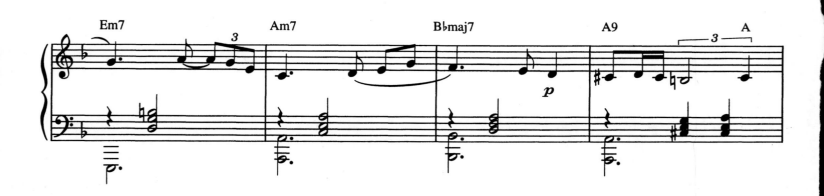

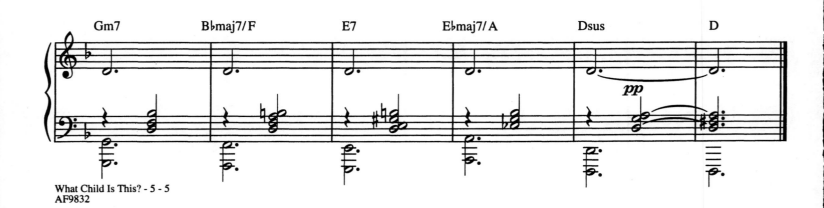